SELF-CONFIDENCE FOR ACTORS

PSYCHOLOGY FOR ACTORS SERIES

ALEXA ISPAS

WORD
BOTHY

CONTENTS

INTRODUCTION

Self-confidence is crucial to having a successful acting career.

When going to auditions, self-confidence tips the odds in your favor.

Even if you are not chosen for the part, a confident performance makes you stand out in the memory of the casting team as a contender for future opportunities.

If you get the part, self-confidence allows you to show up to your first day on the job with genuine enthusiasm, instead of battling imposter syndrome and wondering how long before you get fired.

A confident actor is a joy to work with–for directors, other actors, and the entire production team.

When you are confident, you are not getting in your own way. You are stepping out into the world as you are, instead of a smaller, more insecure version of yourself.

Unfortunately, life as an actor brings out a lot of insecurities.

Your physicality, personality, mannerisms–all these personal aspects of yourself–are exposed to critical evaluation every time you audition for a part, start rehearsals for a new project, or give a performance.

High-pressure situations–an important audition, a table read, or opening night–are times when your self-confidence is most likely to falter.

At such moments, your mind can turn into your biggest enemy.

Instead of allowing you to focus on your performance, it goes on alert and starts scanning for threats–real or imagined.

This sense of threat spreads throughout your body, and before you know it, nerves are getting in the way, disrupting your performance.

At best, such moments are embarrassing yet brief interludes; at worst, they can mark the onset of chronic stage fright.

If this sounds familiar, psychology can help.

Over the past few decades, psychologists have studied the problems associated with low self-confidence and developed a range of simple yet powerful techniques to overcome such barriers.

Self-Confidence for Actors explains in clear and jargon-free language how to apply these psychological insights and tools to your work.

This book explores why you experience difficulties with your self-confidence as an actor.

We delve into the so-called "negativity bias" that governs how your mind interprets information about yourself, especially considering the work actors do.

By understanding how your mind works, you will gain the skills to navigate the self-critical thoughts and feelings that daily life as an actor can generate.

You will also learn a range of simple yet powerful tools to boost your self-confidence, and explore how to apply these tools to the three most common self-confidence problems you are likely to face as an actor: stage fright, battling your inner critic, and imposter syndrome.

In the final chapter, we discuss moments in

your acting career that may challenge your self-confidence, and how to deal with such situations.

I have kept this book short, so you can read it in an afternoon, and gain all the relevant knowledge to perform at your best, both in your day-to-day life and while under pressure.

CHAPTER 1

THE PSYCHOLOGY OF LOW SELF-CONFIDENCE

LOW SELF-CONFIDENCE AS AN ACTOR

Low self-confidence is one of the biggest barriers actors must overcome to build a successful career.

Our brain's so-called "mirror neurons" light up when we watch another person.

If the person we are watching feels uncomfortable, our mirror neurons make us feel uncomfortable too.

When you perform with low self-confidence, your audience cannot relax, which means they cannot enjoy your performance.

In less extreme cases, performing with low self-confidence makes it harder to take creative risks as an actor, leading to a forgettable performance.

Low self-confidence is also visible through poor posture, such as your body contracting in an attempt to hide.

This undermines other people's confidence in you, lowering your chances of success in auditions.

THE NEGATIVITY BIAS

At the root of low self-confidence as an actor lies the so-called "negativity bias."

This bias refers to our tendency as humans to pay disproportionate attention to the negative aspects of our lives.

For example, have you noticed how one bit of criticism can ruin your entire day, while you may receive lots of praise and not even realize it?

Or have you performed worse than usual if you saw one displeased audience member, even though everyone else was having a great time?

The excessive influence of anything negative over your state of mind results from this negativity bias, which has been demonstrated through dozens of psychological studies.

In one of many studies exploring this bias, participants were asked to put on goggles that showed a different image in each eye, a method called "binocular rivalry."

The study showed that participants focused longer on images that evoked fear or disgust than on the more pleasant images.

In another study, participants were given specific information about a student whose face they were examining.

When the information about that student was negative, the participants focused more on the student's face than when the information was positive.

Studies have also shown that the negativity bias starts when we are young.

For example, eight-month-old babies turn quicker to look at the image of a snake than a frog. They are also more likely to turn to see a sad face than a happy face.

As John Tierney and Roy F. Baumeister argue in *The Power of Bad*, the negativity bias affects every area of your life.

Your negative emotions are more impactful and memorable than your positive ones.

You are likely to get more criticism for making mistakes than praise for doing good deeds, and when meeting someone new, a bad first impression has more impact than a good first impression.

It is easier to gain a bad reputation than a good one, and a bad reputation is harder to shake off.

The negativity bias even influences how your body works.

The reflex to withdraw, which comes from the neural signals that travel through your spine, is stronger than the one to advance.

THE POSITIVITY RATIO

To better understand the effects of the negativity bias on your state of mind, it helps to know the extent of this bias.

How many good things does it take to offset one negative thing that comes into your awareness?

Based on research evidence from a variety of sources, Tierney and Baumeister have found there is a so-called "positivity ratio."

For every negative thing that comes to your attention, it takes around four positive things to counteract its effects.

This four-to-one positivity ratio shows how much more weight we attribute to anything negative than anything positive.

In other words, the positivity ratio allows us to estimate how powerfully the negativity bias distorts our perception of reality.

Based on the positivity ratio, anything you do that others judge negatively holds four times more sway than anything positive they notice.

You are also four times more likely to focus on anything negative than anything positive about yourself.

Keeping this four-to-one ratio in mind is essential when evaluating the objectivity of criticisms you receive, or that you direct at yourself.

The positivity ratio also indicates that redressing the balance in the way we view ourselves takes a lot of work.

We will discuss this point in more depth in the next chapter.

THE NEGATIVITY BIAS AND EVOLUTION

If the negativity bias distorts our perception of reality, why is it such a pervasive feature of how our minds work?

When we examine this question through the lens of evolution, we soon realize that the negativity bias has been crucial to our survival.

One mistake can kill you, whereas noticing good things does not save your life.

Paying more attention to threats, such as lions or poisoned berries, than to sources of comfort, kept our ancestors alive long enough to pass on their genes.

The negativity bias also governed how our ancestors lived as members of a community, where one traitorous clan member could prove fatal to everyone else.

Similarly, it made more sense from an evolutionary perspective to pay attention to an enemy's plans of attack than to an ally's kindness.

Even nowadays, when we are safer, healthier, and richer, than our ancestors could have ever hoped to be, we must pay more attention to negative than positive things.

You must remain on alert for cars coming your way, so as not to get hit, and stay on good terms with your colleagues, to avoid getting fired.

As Tierney and Baumeister point out, one loss can erase many previous gains, one act of infidelity can destroy a marriage, and one moment of parental neglect can lead to a lifetime of trauma.

Today, as much as ever, paying extra attention

to the negative aspects of anything in your life makes sense.

The negativity bias is part of being human, and it keeps you safe every day.

The problem is that, as an actor, you can become the focus of your own negativity bias, which can have devastating consequences for your self-confidence.

We will explore this issue in the next chapter.

KEY POINTS

- The "negativity bias" is the tendency to focus a disproportionate amount of attention on anything negative, while ignoring anything positive.
- Psychologists have found that it takes four times as many good things to counteract one negative thing that comes to your awareness.
- Although essential from an evolutionary perspective, the negativity bias creates difficulties for your self-confidence as an actor.

CHAPTER 2

FEELING INSECURE AS AN ACTOR

INSECURITY AND THE ACTING LIFE

Life as an actor brings out a lot of insecurities.

From the moment you decide to pursue acting as a profession, and throughout your career, you are likely to encounter one rejection after another.

When you go to auditions, you face fierce competition from other actors sharing a similar look.

You may also encounter financial difficulties and face long periods of unemployment.

In addition, being an actor places you on the receiving end of criticism more than almost any other profession.

This criticism may come through notes in the

run-up to opening night or scathing professional reviews.

Criticism may also come in less formal ways, such as random bits of conversation you overhear from a costume designer, or interactions on social media.

THE NEGATIVITY BIAS TURNED INWARDS

Given these and many other factors, it is easy to become self-critical and start doubting your every choice.

The more skill and experience you gain as an actor, the more self-critical you become. This affects the way you view yourself.

Because of this overly critical self-focus, the negativity bias directs your attention to all the things that are "wrong" about you—your performance, your looks, your talent, and so on—while ignoring all the positive things.

Instead of scanning your *environment* for threats, *you* become the focus of your own negativity bias.

In addition, as the positivity ratio suggests, any self-critical thought has four times more sway over your sense of self than anything positive you think about yourself.

For example, imagine you come across a negative review of one of your most recent performances.

Restoring your self-confidence after that is not simply a matter of hearing one good thing about yourself, such as reading a positive review.

Based on the positivity ratio, you need as many as four positive reviews, or other positive things, to counteract the effect of that one negative review.

This is why the negativity bias is so insidious, when directed at yourself.

Its effects feel devastating, because your brain pays four times more attention to anything negative than anything positive.

By contrast, if you come across a positive review of your work, it does not give you as much self-confidence as a bad review can take away.

Since your brain is not in the habit of keeping track of positive things, even something as heart-warming as a positive review becomes easy to dismiss from your memory.

As a result, when you make negative self-evaluations, you are likely to be harsher than anyone else.

Over time, you are at risk of losing some of the confidence you had when you started out in the industry, making it harder to perform to your usual standard.

A DISTORTED SENSE OF SELF

The good news is that if you are currently suffering from low self-confidence, most of the negative things you think about yourself do not reflect objective reality.

To counteract these overly self-critical views, you need to start noticing when you are using your negativity bias against yourself.

You also need to understand how your brain interprets information relating to yourself.

By doing so, you can learn how to turn your brain into an ally, instead of allowing it to become your enemy.

The negativity bias works through two so-called "threat detectors" in your brain: the amygdala and the prefrontal cortex.

In the next chapter, we will discuss how these threat detectors affect your sense of self when you turn your negativity bias against yourself.

KEY POINTS

- Life as an actor brings out a lot of insecurities because of various factors, such as constant rejections, the competitive nature of the industry, and frequent criticism.
- Due to these factors, instead of scanning your environment for threats, you become the focus of your own negativity bias.
- The more skill and experience you gain, the more self-critical you become.
- Over time, this critical self-focus can distort your perception of yourself in a way that undermines your self-confidence.

CHAPTER 3

SELF-CONFIDENCE AND YOUR BRAIN

YOUR TWO THREAT DETECTORS

The negativity bias works through two so-called "threat detectors" in your brain: the amygdala and the prefrontal cortex.

Their main purpose is to identify threats, which is how they keep you safe from potential dangers.

The problem is that when you focus these threat detectors on yourself, they flood you with self-critical information, as such information represents a potential "threat," and is therefore deemed to require your full attention.

By contrast, the threat detectors dismiss anything positive they find about you or your performance, as it is irrelevant to their threat-finding focus.

If you are unaware of how they work and do not take action to counteract their impact, these threat detectors can severely undermine your self-confidence as an actor.

THE AMYGDALA: AN ANCIENT PROTECTION MECHANISM

Your first threat detector, the amygdala, is located in the middle of your brain.

This is one of our earliest brain structures as humans and evolved long before language or reasoning.

Your amygdala scans your environment—and yourself, when you are the focus of your negativity bias—for potential threats.

Does the casting director seem confused by your choices? Is there a strange silence as you walk in the room? Is there a stain on your shirt?

In addition to scanning for new threats, the amygdala also looks for any smells, sounds, sights, and other sensory elements linked with past traumatic episodes.

This ancient part of your brain is continuously

"on," and so sensitive, that it often gets triggered before you have any conscious awareness of what is happening.

YOUR AMYGDALA AND THE THREAT RESPONSE

When your amygdala finds a potential danger, it activates a powerful visceral response throughout your body—the so-called "fight-or-flight," or "threat response."

The threat response comes with a multitude of physical manifestations.

Your heart starts pounding, your breathing quickens, your mouth dries up, your hands and knees start shaking, and your digestion shuts down.

With all this activity going on in your body, it becomes difficult to handle anything that requires complex cognitive or motor skills—such as remembering your lines or handling props.

The purpose of the threat response is to save your life. As a result, it happens quickly, with little discrimination between whether or not something is really a danger to your survival.

When your amygdala gets triggered and activates the threat response, your nerves get in the way and you lose focus, which leads to delivering a bad performance.

THE PREFRONTAL CORTEX: THE DANGERS OF ABSTRACTION

Your second threat detector, the prefrontal cortex, covers the front part of your frontal lobe and helps, among other things, with logical reasoning and visualization.

This part of the brain developed much later in our evolution than the amygdala. It is also more complex in humans than in other species.

The prefrontal cortex has several features worth mentioning.

Like the amygdala, your prefrontal cortex searches for any potential threats.

However, unlike the amygdala, the prefrontal cortex does not exclusively rely on your senses in its threat detection process.

Instead, this part of your brain can use your expectations as the basis for creating abstractions that seem real, even though they do not match objective reality.

In other words, your prefrontal cortex does not

only identify something as a threat based on the things you see.

It can also generate an image of something bad happening, perhaps in the future, and provide enough detail to make it seem real.

Another important feature is that when it comes to the neural connections going to your eyes, there are more of these coming from your brain than from the outside world.

This has important implications for how you interpret information relating to yourself.

In particular, when you look at yourself in a self-critical manner, you see what you expect to see.

If you expect to see a problem, this is what your eyes will see, as they are more heavily influenced by your negativity bias than objective reality.

As a result, your negative thoughts and expectations, fueled by the rich imaginative abilities of your prefrontal cortex, can trigger the amygdala as easily as any real danger you encounter.

YOUR PREFRONTAL CORTEX AND SELF-SABOTAGE

If you don't know how to rein in your capacity to catastrophize and imagine all the things that could go wrong, you can terrify yourself with your own thoughts.

For one thing, your prefrontal cortex can zoom in on your tiniest faults, and through its power of visualization, blow them up into huge problems that nobody else notices.

As you see what you expect to see, your prefrontal cortex can also make you paranoid about how your acting choices were received by your director, other members of the production team, or your audience.

And worst of all, because of its influence on the amygdala, your prefrontal cortex can make you imagine all the bad things that could happen during your performance.

These imagined threats can later become self-fulfilling prophecies and mark the onset of chronic stage fright.

SELF-CONFIDENCE AND YOUR THREAT DETECTORS

Your self-confidence depends on the intricate interplay between your two threat detectors: the amygdala and the prefrontal cortex.

If you do not know how to influence this dynamic intentionally, either of these two threat detectors can set in motion a chain of physical reactions that will ruin your performance.

As the amygdala acts impulsively, it can activate the threat response even when there is no real danger.

Alternatively, your prefrontal cortex can push imaginary fears to the forefront of your mind, which can trigger the amygdala to activate the threat response.

Regardless of where the problem starts, the result is always the same: losing focus and delivering a bad performance.

On the other hand, with the right tools and some practice, you can gain control over this powerful dynamic between your amygdala and your prefrontal cortex.

In doing so, you can turn your threat detectors

into empowering allies, as we will discuss in the next chapter.

KEY POINTS

- The negativity bias stems from two so-called "threat detectors" in your brain: the amygdala and the prefrontal cortex.
- When you encounter a potential danger, the amygdala activates the "threat response," a powerful visceral reaction that spreads through your body quickly to save your life.
- The prefrontal cortex, a more sophisticated system concerned with reasoning and visualization, can trigger the amygdala by creating terrifying abstractions that feel real.
- There is a delicate interplay between these two threat detectors, which can lead to self-sabotage.
- On the other hand, with the right tools and some practice, you can turn these threat detectors into your self-confidence allies.

CHAPTER 4

NURTURING YOUR SELF-CONFIDENCE

COUNTERING THE NEGATIVITY BIAS

Most of the negative things you currently think about yourself do not reflect objective reality.

They are the result of how your two threat detectors–the amygdala and the prefrontal cortex–interpret information about yourself, continuously strengthening your negativity bias.

If you want to counteract the negative effect of these two threat detectors on your self-confidence, you need to put in a significant amount of work.

In addition, with the right tools and some practice, you can turn your threat detectors into powerful self-confidence allies.

CALMING YOUR AMYGDALA

As the amygdala is one of your oldest brain structures, it evolved long before language.

This means you cannot talk yourself out of the threat response once it gets activated.

The only way to calm your amygdala, and prevent the threat response from ruining your performance, is to work directly with your body.

In high-pressure situations, such as before opening night, or when going to an important audition, you need to calm your amygdala.

You may not be able to stop the threat response from getting activated, but you can learn to tone it down to a manageable level through targeted body-focused tools.

These tools must work quickly and rely on minimal cognitive processing.

Simplicity is important, because when the amygdala gets triggered, you have low cognitive resources at your disposal.

In addition, you can learn how to project confidence through your body language, which makes a great first impression and puts your audience at ease.

TURNING YOUR PREFRONTAL CORTEX INTO AN ALLY

Despite the negative effects your prefrontal cortex can have on your self-confidence, you can turn this part of your brain into an ally if you know how to work with it.

You can train your prefrontal cortex to bring your attention to positive things about yourself.

Your prefrontal cortex is already excellent at searching and identifying things about you.

The problem is that, because of the negativity bias, these are currently aspects of your appearance and personality that make you feel bad about yourself.

To increase your self-confidence, you need to train your prefrontal cortex to look for positive things, such as endearing traits and past successes.

Your prefrontal cortex will still search for negative things, because this is not something it can stop doing.

However, through conscious effort, you can train this part of your brain to also identify and highlight positive things.

These positive aspects will counteract any self-critical thoughts and boost your self-confidence.

Another way your prefrontal cortex can become your ally is through the use of logic.

Unlike the amygdala, your prefrontal cortex is open to rational thinking and verbal instructions.

Once you understand the origin of your fears, you can talk yourself out of them by challenging your fear-based thoughts with logical reasoning.

By reassuring yourself in this way, you will experience less fear and your body will calm down.

To strengthen the calming effect of your prefrontal cortex, you can visualize your performance going well.

This activates an empowering emotional state, boosting your self-confidence.

Athletes often use such positive visualizations to prepare for competitions, just as you can use them to get ready for your performance.

Encouraging your prefrontal cortex to help you imagine things going well may require some practice.

However, the more you train your prefrontal cortex towards positive visual imaginings, the more impact these will have on your state of mind.

DEVELOPING A RANGE OF TOOLS

To maintain a good level of self-confidence as an actor, you need to learn how to work with your two threat detectors, your amygdala and your prefrontal cortex.

The more skilled you become at working with these threat detectors intentionally, the easier it will be to counteract the effect of the negativity bias on your self-confidence.

With practice, you can train your brain to pay attention to the positive things about you and your performance.

Over the next two chapters, you will learn a range of tools that will allow you to calm your amygdala and harness the helpful features of your prefrontal cortex.

KEY POINTS

- You need lots of conscious effort, and a range of tools, to counteract the impact of your threat detectors on your self-confidence.

- When you find yourself under pressure, you need to learn how to calm your amygdala.
- To restore a healthy sense of self and boost your self-confidence in your day-to-day life, you also need to train your prefrontal cortex to look for positive things about you and your performance.

CHAPTER 5

SELF-CONFIDENCE AND YOUR BODY

PREPARING YOUR BODY

In this chapter, you will learn five body-focused tools designed to help you tone down the threat response and radiate self-confidence even when under pressure.

The body-focused tools you will find in this chapter are extremely simple. However, do not be fooled by their simplicity.

They are fast-acting and effective at calming the amygdala, which is non-verbal.

These body tools also help you project confidence through the way you use your body.

This will help you make a great first impression

and allow anyone watching your performance to relax and enjoy themselves.

THE FIVE BODY-FOCUSED TOOLS

I suggest you use these body-focused tools in the order in which I introduce them.

When you use them in this order, they follow a natural progression towards helping you restore balance in your body.

However, it is important that you tailor this process to your needs.

If you find that a different order works better for you, or you would like to ignore some tools and focus on others, adapt them to your specific requirements.

The first two tools will prevent the threat response from spreading throughout your body.

The other three tools will give your body a sense of empowerment and presence, allowing you to perform at your best.

Regulate your breath

As soon as you sense the threat response becoming active in your body, it is time to use the first tool: regulating your breath.

Start by focusing on your outbreath, as it is easier to push breath out than to take breath in, especially when you are in a state of alert.

Push your breath out and count to four.

Hold for four counts.

Then allow the breath to come back into your body for four counts. Do not force this to happen; simply allow it.

Keep doing this for as long as it takes to feel calmer and more in control of your body.

Do not be put off by the simplicity of this tool. When your cognitive resources are low, as they are when your body is in "fight or flight" mode, simplicity is what you need.

There is no quicker or more effective way to stop the threat response from spreading throughout your body than focusing on your breath.

By regulating your breath, you are lowering your heart rate; this is why this tool is so effective.

Lowering your heart rate is key, because your heart beating faster sets in motion the other elements of the threat response.

While you cannot control your heart rate, you can influence it through your breath.

Regulating your breath leads to your heart rate going down, which will prevent the other aspects of the threat response from becoming activated.

Use your feet as your foundation

Once you feel your body calming down, it is time to bring out your second body-focused tool: using your feet as your foundation.

This second tool, like the first, is also simple, yet effective and fast-acting.

Make sure the soles of your feet are fully on the ground, whether you are standing or sitting.

If the situation allows, spread your legs about a hip-width apart, to give yourself maximum stability.

The aim is to become as grounded as possible in your body, using your feet as your foundation.

You can enhance the effectiveness of this tool by adding a powerful visualization of yourself as a tree, with your feet connecting you deep into the earth.

You will feel stable in yourself, which–coupled with a steady breath and a slow heart rate—will allow you to stay fully present and grounded.

This tool also helps you gather and contain your energy, so try to remain as still as possible while using it.

Resist the urge to pace or do anything else that would aggravate your nerves.

Finding stability in your body will boost your confidence, which in turn will give others confidence in you.

Activate your confidence anchor

The third body-focused tool consists of creating a touch anchor in your body, which we will call your "confidence anchor."

A touch anchor is a specific point on your body that you learn to associate with a state of being—in this case, self-confidence.

This simple yet powerful technique is used in certain therapeutic settings, such as hypnotherapy, and is highly effective, with practice.

When feeling under pressure, a touch anchor can help you boost your self-confidence.

You can create this anchor right now, so it will be ready to use when you need it.

Make sure you are in a neutral state of mind as you create your confidence anchor; not too agitated, nor too disengaged.

For this technique, it is best to use your non-dominant hand. This means that if you are right-handed, you should use your left hand, and the other way around if you are left-handed.

Use the tip of your thumb to find the first knuckle of your middle finger, which is where we will place the confidence anchor.

Touch that spot with your thumb a few times, to bring your full attention to it.

Spend a few minutes remembering a moment when you felt fully confident.

Remember how your body felt and recall as many details about that moment as you can.

For example, how old were you?

What were you wearing?

What could you see, as you were looking out into the world?

Re-experience that moment as vividly as you can, allowing your whole body to rejoice.

When your self-confidence is at its peak, press your thumb against your anchor.

Then take your thumb off the anchor and allow yourself time to get back to neutral.

I will now ask you to do something that will distract you from what you were doing: say the digits of your phone number in reverse order.

Once you have done that, touch your confidence anchor. Can you notice your self-confidence going up again?

The feeling is likely to be subtle at first, but the more you use your anchor, the more powerful its effect on your body will be.

Over the next few days, keep recalling moments when you felt a high level of self-confidence.

Whenever you find a powerful memory, touch your confidence anchor.

This will strengthen the effect of your anchor, as all these memories will become associated with that one spot on your body.

Make your body bigger

Once you have used your confidence anchor and have brought a strong feeling of self-confidence into your body, it is time to use the fourth tool, which is to project this feeling of self-confidence outwards by making your body bigger.

In the animal kingdom, animals use their body

to signal their confidence level.

When they feel confident, they make their body bigger. Making their body smaller signals a lack of confidence.

As humans, we do this as well.

When we win a competition, we spread our arms out in victory or put our hands on our hips and puff out our chest.

On the other hand, when our confidence is low, we contract our body in an attempt to hide.

The interesting thing about this instinctual behavior is that it also works the other way around.

By making your body bigger, you can increase your self-confidence.

One of the easiest ways to do so is to spend at least a couple of minutes in the so-called "super(wo)man pose."

This pose consists of standing with your legs spread a hip-width apart and your hands on your hips, staring straight ahead.

The super(wo)man pose makes your body bigger and gives the signal, "I am a winner."

Holding this pose for a couple of minutes initiates changes in your body and mind that boost your self-confidence.

The effects of the super(wo)man pose were

demonstrated by psychology researcher Amy Cuddy.

Her experimental studies show that our body language affects how we think and feel about ourselves.

In one of her studies, participants sat either in the super(wo)man pose or in a low-power pose (leaning inwards, legs crossed) for two minutes.

The results showed that those participants who sat in the super(wo)man pose felt more powerful, and performed better in mock interviews, than the participants in the low-power pose group.

In another study, Amy Cuddy demonstrated that power posing influences hormones, which may be the reason it is so effective at boosting self-confidence.

Participants who did power posing had an increase in testosterone and a decrease in cortisol, two effects that are linked with self-confidence.

I recommend watching Amy Cuddy's excellent TED talk on power posing, in which she explains how and why it is effective, and reading her book *Presence*.

While waiting to audition, use the super(wo)man pose to boost your self-confidence.

If it would be too awkward, given the circumstances, to do this physically, visualize yourself striking this pose.

In addition, consider all other available ways to make your body bigger.

If possible, stand rather than sit while waiting.

If you must sit, use alternative ways to make your body bigger.

For example, wrap your arms around the back of a chair to ensure that you open your chest and shoulders.

You can also use objects in your environment to make your body bigger.

For example, if you are standing, you can rest your arm on a chair.

If you have lines to look at before an audition, hold them in a way that prevents you from collapsing your arms and body.

Watch out for pinning your upper arms from armpit to elbow at your sides, a posture called "penguin arms," as this makes you contract your body instead of making it bigger.

The more confident you look in your body during high-pressure moments, such as during an audition, the more you will put anyone watching at ease, which will allow them to enjoy your performance.

Reframe nerves as excitement

It is natural to feel nervous in high-pressure situations, even after using the previous four body-focused tools.

Aiming for total calm is pointless, so do not tell yourself to "calm down."

Besides, nervousness is not a bad thing.

If you keep your nerves to a manageable level, being slightly tense can help you be more present during your performance.

To ensure that your nerves do not get in the way, use the fifth tool: tell yourself, "I am excited," instead of, "I am nervous."

Excitement and nervousness have similar physiological characteristics, which is something you can use to your advantage.

Telling yourself that you are excited will put a positive label on what you are experiencing in your body.

This positive label will feel encouraging and motivating, leading to a better performance.

APPLYING THE BODY-FOCUSED TOOLS

As previously mentioned, the body-focused tools in this chapter are simple, which is what makes them so effective.

Use the body-focused tools before every performance, even those you do not feel nervous about.

The more you use these tools, the more effective they become.

With practice, these tools will become second nature, and your body will know how to tone down the threat response if it gets activated.

This means you will restore your balance quickly, preventing nerves from sabotaging your performance.

If there is any tool you do not feel comfortable using when you are in a public place, you can visualize yourself using it.

Over time, your visualizations will have a similar effect to physically using the tools.

In addition to these body-focused tools, you can use mind-focused tools to improve your focus while performing and increase your self-confidence long-term.

In the next chapter, you will learn six tools to increase your self-confidence using your mind.

KEY POINTS

- The body-focused tools are simple, fast-acting, and effective at preventing the threat response from spreading throughout your body.
- As body and mind are linked, these tools also increase your self-confidence by using your body to influence your mental state.
- Regulate your breath. Push your breath out and count to four, hold for four counts, then allow breath to come back into your body for four counts. This will slow down your heart rate, which is how the threat response gets started in the body.
- Use your feet as your foundation. This will help you feel stable in your body and contain your energy, so that you can channel it into your performance.
- Activate your confidence anchor. You can create a strong anchor point on your body that you can use whenever you need a self-confidence boost.

- Make your body bigger. This further increases your self-confidence and helps you make a great first impression.
- Reframe nerves as excitement. Use the word "excitement" when describing your physiological state to yourself and others.

CHAPTER 6

SELF-CONFIDENCE AND YOUR MIND

TURNING YOUR MIND INTO AN ALLY

Now that you have a set of tools to tone down the threat response and bring a feeling of self-confidence into your body, it is time to turn our attention to your mind.

In this chapter, you will learn six mind-focused tools you can use to increase your self-confidence.

These mind-focused tools are slower acting than the body-focused tools in the previous chapter.

Their value lies in eliminating negative self-talk, allowing you to focus on your performance.

In addition, the mind-focused tools will increase your self-confidence when dealing with challenging day-to-day situations by helping you take conscious control of your thoughts.

Just as the body tools primarily focus on your amygdala, the mind tools are mainly designed to work with your prefrontal cortex.

As previously mentioned, the prefrontal cortex is the part of your brain concerned with logical reasoning and visualization.

By allowing you to imagine what might happen in the future, the prefrontal cortex helps you prepare so you can avoid danger.

However, because of this feature, your prefrontal cortex can flood your brain with horror-inducing images of threats that will never materialize.

This part of your brain can turn into your enemy if left unchecked, but also holds great potential for increasing your self-confidence if you know how to work with it.

The tools you will learn in this chapter will help you turn your prefrontal cortex into a self-confidence ally.

THE SIX MIND-FOCUSED TOOLS

Each of the six mind-focused tools is particularly useful in certain situations.

Some of these tools address the way you talk to yourself, others are about things you visualize before an important day.

Unlike the body-focused tools, you can use the mind-focused tools in whatever order feels right for you.

You can also select the most relevant ones for each situation you find yourself in.

The more you practice, the more effective these tools become, and the more you will find yourself using positive, empowering self-talk.

As a result of regularly using these tools, your self-confidence will improve.

Your unique selling points

One of the most important aspects of self-confidence is knowing yourself. This also applies when it comes to your self-confidence as an actor.

For this reason, the "unique selling points" tool can profoundly impact your self-confidence throughout your acting career.

Keep this tool at the back of your mind as you consider which parts to audition for and which projects to take on.

To identify your unique selling points, ask yourself a few important questions:

- What do you bring to the table as an actor?
- How would a director who enjoys working with you describe you to a colleague?
- What kinds of stories can you tell through your physicality?

These questions may sound basic, but it is amazing how many actors waste a lot of effort pursuing opportunities that are not right for them.

As a result, they increase the number of rejections they get, which undermines their self-confidence.

Even when they get cast, being in a part that is not a great fit means they can only deliver a disappointing performance, lowering their chances of future success.

By being clear on what you bring to the table, you will make better career decisions.

Understanding the kinds of stories you can tell through your physical presence will help you focus your efforts on auditioning for parts that are a good fit.

When you do, you will have better chances of success, which will increase your self-confidence.

In addition, when you get cast, you will have a sense of belonging and alignment, leading to a better performance.

Regularly reminding yourself of your unique selling points will make it easier to find the right people and environments for you.

In such environments, you won't need to pretend and make yourself fit whatever expectations are placed upon you.

Instead, you will shine by simply being who you are.

Your pride smoothie

Because of the negativity bias, things we are proud of are easy to forget.

The pride smoothie is a simple tool that serves two important purposes: it retrains your brain to focus on things you do well, and it helps you keep track of these things over time.

At the end of each day, take a few minutes to write in your journal three things you did that you are proud of; this is your "pride smoothie."

The three things do not have to be acting-related. They can be anything you feel proud of, such as doing yoga, responding well to a setback, or fulfilling a promise to yourself.

The pride smoothie's positive impact is cumulative.

By using this tool every day, you are training your brain, particularly your prefrontal cortex, to pay attention to the things you do well.

Over time, your brain will more readily notice these things and your self-confidence will grow.

In addition, by providing yourself with this much-needed acknowledgment, you will require less praise from others.

You will therefore be more fun to be around, because you will be less focused on yourself.

Any acknowledgment from others will feel like a bonus rather than a necessity.

This tool requires discipline and consistency, but it is easy to use.

Once you use it a few times, and see how good it makes you feel, you will be motivated to keep going.

As an added benefit, using the daily pride smoothie will motivate you to do things you are proud of, so you have good things to report.

Your greatest hits

Your "greatest hits" are moments in your life when you felt successful and accomplished.

Make a list of any such times you remember, even small moments of success that make you feel good.

You can acknowledge times when you have been generous to others, or clever at coming up with solutions to a problem.

Include moments when you realized you had improved as an actor, and moments that made you a more rounded human being.

This list is a valuable resource for growing your self-confidence.

Put this list somewhere you can easily access.

Whenever you need a self-confidence boost, read this list, one item at a time.

When reading this list, remember all the sensory details of the moments you have listed.

Read this list every morning before an audition, to remind yourself of all your past successes.

You can even take this list with you to auditions and read it while waiting. It will help you stay grounded and boost your self-confidence.

Over time, as you experience more amazing moments, remember to update your list.

Your ideal day

Let us turn our attention to your visual system and how to harness its potential.

We will concentrate on your ability to plan, which is regulated in great part by your prefrontal cortex.

You already use this forward-thinking ability unconsciously when you let anxiety-provoking scenarios run through your mind.

Using the "ideal day" tool, you can take conscious control of your brain's ability to envision possible futures.

For example, on the morning of an important day, take some time to envision everything going perfectly.

What would that day look like?

Put as much detail into your envisioning as you can, and make it positive.

I am guessing you have done these kinds of

visualizations before and have already experienced how powerful they can be.

If so, let me introduce you to a simple yet powerful addition: learning to associate with the images you see, as you go through your visualization.

By "associating" with an image, I mean seeing it as if you were present at that moment, experiencing it in all its intensity, instead of seeing the image from a distance, like a movie.

When you visualize your perfect day, make sure you are doing so in an associated way.

Fully experience what it will be like to have such a great day, with everything working out.

For example, how confident would you feel if you turned up to an important audition and all the members of the casting team looked delighted as soon as you walked in the room?

What if they told you that you look perfect for the part and they have already heard great things about your work?

Come up with as many positive images and possibilities as you can.

Then walk through your visualization as if all this is really happening.

In this way, you are setting yourself up for

success and helping your body relax once you start your actual day.

The auditory swish

The auditory swish will help you get rid of negative self-talk, the kind that often comes up when battling your inner critic or imposter syndrome.

This self-talk consists of outdated voices from your past.

You have probably outgrown these voices, but some auditory remnants are still lingering in your consciousness.

Such remnants may include self-judgments, such as, "I am lazy," or limiting beliefs, such as, "Nothing good ever happens to me."

This negative self-talk fragments your consciousness and makes it difficult to focus on your performance.

It also puts you in danger of forgetting your lines, because it uses the part of your brain that is needed for speech.

To get rid of this self-talk, pick a negative thought that comes into your mind and allow yourself to become curious about it.

Is there any specific voice attached to it? If so, is it your voice, or does the voice belong to someone else? Can you recognize whose voice it is?

If you recognize the voice, it helps to reflect on your relationship with that person, and how this person has shaped your development.

Perhaps this was someone you knew while growing up, when you felt more vulnerable than at present.

It may be that you now have a different view of your relationship than you did at the time, and can see any problematic patterns you may have been oblivious to in the past.

Seeing the relationship from your current perspective may help to reduce the voice's negative impact on your state of mind.

It is now time to get rid of this left-over negative self-talk.

I will introduce you to two methods of doing it, and I encourage you to experiment and find out which works best for you.

The first method is to change the voice from what it is, which is likely to be serious, to something funny, that sounds like a cartoon character.

Have fun with this. The more ridiculous the voice, the better.

Practice this method whenever you hear negative self-talk. Notice the words gradually losing their impact.

The second method is more in-depth, but it works well for any kind of self-talk, even the kind that does not have a specific voice attached to it.

Imagine you have a remote control, which you can use to change the volume of thoughts that come into your mind.

As soon as you hear the negative self-talk, press the volume control button on your remote to make the words fade out.

Practice this for a while, until you get better at it.

Imagine there is a "you" out there who does not have this negative self-talk going through their mind.

See that person looking at you and saying something positive and uplifting.

They could say, "You are safe," or whatever you need to hear, that would give you confidence.

Focus on these positive words and soak them in.

The final step is to hear the sound of the sea washing it all away, before repeating this process as many times as you need.

You will soon notice your negative self-talk decreasing in both frequency and viciousness.

Eventually, it will no longer interfere with your ability to perform, making it easier to do your best in high-pressure situations.

Reducing negative self-talk will also have a positive effect on your self-confidence day-to-day.

The positivity ratio

As you know by now through learning about the negativity bias, your brain has a natural tendency to focus on negative rather than positive things.

Given that, as an actor, you are forced to focus much of your attention on yourself, you experience this negativity bias turned inwards, which makes you overly self-critical.

It is important to counteract this self-critical tendency by taking conscious control of your thoughts, particularly those relating to yourself.

Fortunately, you now have the ideal tool: the positivity ratio.

Based on the positivity ratio, it takes four positive things to counteract one negative thing.

This ratio is a powerful tool in your arsenal, as it gives you a concrete goal to reach for.

Remind yourself of this ratio whenever something damages your self-confidence, such as receiving hurtful notes from your director.

It is likely that the hurt was caused by the negativity bias—both in how the director delivered the notes and in how you interpreted them.

To counteract the effect of the negativity bias on your self-confidence, you can learn to use the positivity ratio to your advantage.

Every time you have a negative thought about yourself, spend time thinking of four positive things to counteract the negative thought.

Don't be too picky in choosing these four things. They can be simple, such as, "I am polite, always turn up on time, know how to take care of myself, and have good skin."

As you keep using the positivity ratio to counteract the effects of the negativity bias, your brain will get into the habit of looking for positive things even without your conscious intent.

You can also use the positivity ratio if you are confronted by a negative comment about yourself on social media.

To avoid damaging your self-confidence, scroll

away from that comment and read four positive things people have said about you.

APPLYING THE MIND-FOCUSED TOOLS

Each of the tools works with certain aspects of your brain, especially your prefrontal cortex.

For example, the "ideal day" tool is designed to work with the visual aspect of your brain, the auditory swish with the acoustic aspect, and so on.

You will need some of these tools more frequently than others, depending on how your mind works.

For example, if you are a visual person and you "see" horrendous scenarios in your mind's eye that make you lose focus during your performance, the "ideal day" tool will be one you will use a great deal.

You may also find some tools more useful than others at various points in your career.

For example, if you frequently find yourself in the public eye, you may find the positivity ratio especially helpful.

Over time, certain problems will become less significant, while others may disappear completely.

Whatever your circumstances, you now have a

range of tools you can use to stay focused on your performance.

As with the body tools, learning to apply the mind tools requires time and practice.

Putting in the effort to master these tools will not only help your acting career; it will also provide you with important life skills.

Over the next three chapters, we will discuss how to put these mind-focused tools, as well as the body-focused tools in the previous chapter, into practice.

You will learn to apply the tools to the three most common self-confidence challenges actors face: stage fright, inner critic interference, and imposter syndrome.

Although these three challenges often compound each other, for the purpose of clarity, we will address them in individual chapters, starting with stage fright.

KEY POINTS

- The six mind-focused tools aim to turn your prefrontal cortex into your self-confidence ally.

- Your unique selling points. Identify what you bring to the table as an actor, to make better career decisions.

- Your pride smoothie. At the end of each day, take a few minutes to write in your journal three things you did that you are proud of.

- Your greatest hits. Make a list of your biggest successes, to remind yourself of all the amazing things you have already accomplished.

- Your ideal day. Before important days, visualize everything going as well as possible and allow your body to experience the joy of this perfect day.

- The auditory swish will help you get rid of negative self-talk, the kind that is associated with the inner critic or imposter syndrome.

- The positivity ratio. For every negative thing you think about yourself, find four positive things to counteract the effect of the negativity bias on your self-confidence.

CHAPTER 7

OVERCOMING STAGE FRIGHT

STAGE FRIGHT AND THE ACTING LIFE

Stage fright is characterized by an activation of the threat response when performing in front of others.

This is the most visible and well-known aspect of struggling with your self-confidence as an actor, showing up as a range of debilitating physical symptoms before or during a performance.

Even if you have not experienced stage fright, it is important to have a process for dealing with it, in case it arises at some point during the course of your career.

Taking the time to think through the chain of events that lead to the onset of stage fright gives you the ability to intervene before stage fright becomes chronic and affects your ability to perform.

STAGE FRIGHT AS PERFORMANCE ANXIETY

Although the manifestations of stage fright are often similar from one person to another, the causes of stage fright can be different.

The most common cause is a visceral fear that arises when performing in front of others–an affliction also referred to as "performance anxiety."

If you suffer from this type of stage fright, it is important to realize that your fear is perfectly normal and has its roots in our evolutionary history.

Our ancestors had a visceral fear of being watched by a predator in the dark, as this would mark them out as prey.

Without this fear, humans would not have survived; it is understandable that this fear is still present in our psyche.

The experience of stepping out on stage, as audience members watch you quietly from the darkness of the auditorium, stokes this primal fear.

To address this fear, spend time calming your amygdala before every performance.

Use the body-focused tools in chapter 5 and anything else you find soothing.

In addition, if you experience this type of stage fright, a good memorization process is key.

You must learn your lines so well that they roll off your tongue, requiring minimal effort during the performance.

In my book *Memorization for Actors*, I have outlined a memorization process that can help you remember your lines even when under pressure.

If you are looking for an effective memorization process to help with stage fright, I recommend you check out that book.

STAGE FRIGHT AND SENSITIZATION

A less well-known yet no less debilitating type of stage fright can set in after having performed many years without a problem, or in the middle of a show you have done hundreds of times.

This second type of stage fright is caused by the so-called "sensitization" process.

Sensitization often starts with experiencing a brief moment of trauma while on stage, such as dropping a prop or momentarily forgetting your lines.

This can happen in the middle of a long show run, when you become so used to doing the show that you almost perform on automatic pilot.

Unfortunately, this is when you are most at risk of experiencing this type of traumatic event.

The moment may go unnoticed by the audience, but to you, it is likely to feel catastrophic.

During that moment, your amygdala becomes sensitized to any sensory elements you encountered before the trauma.

This may include the smell of backstage, the bright lights, or even the walk from your dressing room.

Once you become sensitized, these sensory elements turn into triggers that activate the threat response any time you encounter them.

If you find yourself in this situation, it is important to realize that you are not alone–far from it.

There is a stigma attached to experiencing stage fright, and many actors feel ashamed if they suffer from it.

As such, actors rarely admit to battling stage fright, and often make it even worse before they seek help.

If you are suffering from stage fright caused by

sensitization, work with a therapist to identify and overcome your stage fright triggers.

I also recommend reading *Facing the Fear*, an excellent book on this type of stage fright written by Bella Merlin, who discusses relevant research and her own experience of overcoming stage fright.

Many actors have successfully gone through the de-sensitization process and have been able to return to the stage.

SELF-CONFIDENCE WHEN DEALING WITH STAGE FRIGHT

Whether the stage fright is of the "performance anxiety" kind or caused by sensitization, working with your body is essential to overcoming it.

In chapter 5, we explored several tools you can use for that purpose.

In using these tools, it is important to emphasize the role of preparing your body before every performance.

The purpose of this preparation is to prevent the threat response from becoming activated, or to tone it down if it does get triggered, instead of waiting until you feel too overwhelmed to intervene.

If your stage fright becomes overwhelming and affects your performance, remember that your body is trying to protect you. Be kind to it, and forgive yourself.

Once you start overcoming your stage fright, do not set the unrealistic goal of complete calm.

Having nerves before a performance is normal, even once you start making progress.

Make sure you approach this process with an optimistic mindset. Your stage fright is not permanent.

It is something you can change, as long as you keep practicing and allow for the possibility of change.

Your brain is malleable and can learn, if given enough opportunities to practice.

The more you practice, the more the tools will become second nature.

Remember that the audience is on your side. They are not predators watching you from the dark, waiting for you to fail.

They want you to give a good performance, and their mirror neurons make them feel empathic towards you. If you succeed, so do they.

Your negativity bias will direct your attention towards the most critical audience members.

To counteract this tendency, redirect your focus towards enthusiastic members of your audience, those who make you feel good about yourself and your performance.

Speak kindly to yourself at all times, even on days when your performance does not go as well as you would have liked.

By being gentle and nurturing towards yourself, you are calming your amygdala and giving yourself the opportunity to grow your self-confidence day by day.

In the next chapter, we will address the way you talk to yourself in more depth by exploring another challenging aspect of low self-confidence: your inner critic.

KEY POINTS

- Stage fright is the most well-known and visible barrier to self-confidence as an actor. It shows up as a range of debilitating physical symptoms before or during your performance.
- This fear is often caused by an evolutionary dread of being watched.

- Stage fright can also set in later in your acting career. In such cases, it is caused by so-called "sensitization" during a moment of trauma. This leads to previously harmless sensory elements turning into debilitating triggers.
- Regardless of its origin, it is possible to overcome stage fright by calming your amygdala and using positive self-talk to nurture your confidence.

CHAPTER 8

DISARMING YOUR INNER CRITIC

YOUR INNER CRITIC

Your so-called "inner critic" refers to negative self-talk that makes you feel insecure about yourself.

This self-talk can show up in many ways, but generally speaking, it is highly judgmental and leaves no room for appreciating the positive things about yourself.

When you turn your negativity bias against yourself, your inner critic jumps into self-sabotaging action.

Your inner critic may criticize your appearance, choices, talent, or any other personal attributes you feel insecure about.

It may show up through negative thoughts

about yourself, such as, "I'm lazy," "I'm a rubbish actor," or, "I never get anything right."

The inner critic can also show up as negatively comparing yourself with another actor, making you doubt your acting choices, or highlighting all the ways you didn't prepare enough for your performance. Ironically, this takes up valuable preparation time.

Given all these negative effects, the inner critic makes you want to hide, instead of being seen.

This can lead to an awkward performance as your posture contracts, reflecting your state of mind.

THE INNER CRITIC AND SELF-SABOTAGE

Because of the negativity bias, if you look for faults in yourself or your performance, you will find them.

Your brain is primed to remind you of your faults, which keeps your inner critic active and energized.

In addition, as we know from the positivity ratio, anything negative you find counts four times more than anything positive.

You may think that your inner critic is

protecting you from making mistakes, but in reality, it sabotages you by lowering your self-confidence and fragmenting your focus.

Because of its perfectionistic standards, your inner critic inhibits your playfulness and makes you hold back from taking creative risks.

The perfectionistic mindset the inner critic generates makes every mistake seem like a major setback.

While performing, your inner critic makes you lose focus, overwhelms your cognitive resources, and puts you in danger of forgetting your lines.

This is because your inner critic is harder on you, and more hurtful, than any outside critic.

Even in mild cases, your inner critic distracts you from being fully present as you perform and makes you doubt yourself.

Reminding yourself of your inner critic's self-sabotaging impact will help you shake off its influence and develop a healthy sense of self.

SELF-CONFIDENCE AND YOUR INNER CRITIC

The inner critic generally shows up in an auditory way, often through outdated voices from your past.

This could be the voice of a critical parent, a coach intent on "breaking" you, or a bully.

It is like an auditory script you downloaded from those who seemed more powerful and knowing than you.

The good news is that, as you may have discovered in chapter 6, you can use the auditory swish to "erase" these outdated voices from your mind.

In addition, using some of the other mind-focused tools in chapter 6, you can direct your attention towards positive things about yourself and your performance.

In doing so, you are encouraging your brain to pay less attention to anything negative and more attention to your positive attributes.

Your prefrontal cortex can help in this task.

Even though it is slower at finding positive than negative things, and training it to find positive things requires conscious effort, this can become second nature with time and practice.

Use the positivity ratio to your advantage.

Set the goal of identifying four positive things about yourself for every self-critical thought.

In addition, keep reminding yourself of your "greatest hits," and spend a few minutes every day filling up on your "pride smoothie."

Give yourself lots of time and patience in going through this process.

It is not easy to change your habitual thought patterns, especially as the negativity bias is such an integral part of how our brains work.

However, with the right tools and lots of practice, you will gradually weaken your inner critic's negative influence on your self-confidence.

As you do, you will notice having fewer self-critical intrusive thoughts and maintain better focus during your performance.

You will also find it easier to soothe yourself when facing outside criticism, as you won't spend as much energy afterwards battling your inner critic's even harsher comments.

In the next chapter, we will discuss how to overcome "imposter syndrome," which often allows your inner critic to cause even more damage to your self-confidence.

KEY POINTS

- The term "inner critic" refers to self-talk that makes you feel insecure about yourself.

- Because of the negativity bias, if you look for faults in yourself or your performance, as the inner critic encourages you to do, you will find them.
- Based on the positivity ratio, every fault has four times more impact on your state of mind than anything positive you find.
- You can counteract your inner critic's influence on your self-confidence by using the auditory swish to erase any unhelpful inner voices.
- You can also use some of the other mind tools to remind yourself about your positive attributes.
- Give yourself lots of time and patience when going through this process, as changing your habitual thought patterns is not an easy task.

CHAPTER 9

CONQUERING IMPOSTER SYNDROME

IMPOSTER SYNDROME

"Imposter syndrome" refers to feeling like a fraud and wondering how long it will take before others start noticing your inadequacy.

As an actor, you are most likely to experience imposter syndrome when you get a career boost.

For example, you may experience imposter syndrome when your hard work finally pays off and you get cast in a dream role.

You may have spent so long hoping for something like this to happen that when it finally does, the threat of losing this opportunity feels terrifying.

In this type of situation, the negativity bias will

draw your attention to all the reasons you are not right for the role.

Instead of celebrating your accomplishment, you will think of all the actors who could do this job better than you.

Alternatively, you may experience imposter syndrome after coming back to acting following a hiatus and wondering if everyone can tell how insecure you feel.

IMPOSTER SYNDROME AND SELF-SABOTAGE

Imposter syndrome has many negative consequences, including comparing yourself negatively to other actors and feeling the urge to hide.

Instead of enjoying your hard-earned success or taking decisive action, you are battling intrusive thoughts that fragment your focus.

You are also likely to imagine all the ways you could fail, and all the disastrous consequences this would have for the future.

As your posture is likely to reflect your lack of confidence and undermine other people's confidence in you, these fears can become self-fulfilling prophecies.

The possibility of humiliation is often a primary trigger for imposter syndrome.

Your brain is trying to protect you, but doing so in a misguided way, which leads to self-sabotage.

The inner critic often compounds the effect of imposter syndrome on your self-confidence.

Once you start thinking of yourself as a fraud, your inner critic will articulate all the reasons this is the case.

This combination of feeling like an imposter and battling your inner critic is debilitating, making it difficult to show up in the world as you really are.

Instead, when battling these inner demons, you will only be able to reveal a small and insecure version of yourself.

In extreme circumstances, experiencing imposter syndrome may even activate the threat response, letting nerves get in the way of your performance.

SELF-CONFIDENCE AND IMPOSTER SYNDROME

Whenever you find yourself battling imposter syndrome, remind yourself that your thinking is influenced by the negativity bias.

In particular, remember that as an actor, you are naturally inclined to focus your negativity bias inwards, distorting the way you see yourself.

As such, your self-critical thoughts do not reflect objective reality or the way others see you.

Reminding yourself of the way your brain distorts your self-perception will make it easier to challenge the self-critical thoughts triggering your imposter syndrome.

To take this challenge one step further, give yourself something to argue with: real evidence.

Make a list of the reasons you are suited for this opportunity.

To make this list even more persuasive, write down all the unique qualities you bring to the table.

Putting all these pieces of evidence in writing is a powerful way to re-direct your mind away from self-sabotage.

In doing so, you will remind yourself you are not a fraud and deserve all the good things coming your way.

By writing this list, you will harness the power of your prefrontal cortex as your self-confidence ally.

Instead of bombarding you with scenarios of

public humiliation, your prefrontal cortex will start paying closer attention to all the points in your favor.

To relieve any lingering anxieties, talk about your imposter syndrome with close friends, or a therapist specializing in this area.

Talking to others will help you realize that you are not alone in battling imposter syndrome; it is a common problem, especially among actors.

In addition, remember to use the body and mind tools you learned throughout this book.

If you only have time to use one tool, go through your "greatest hits," to remind yourself of all the reasons you are amazing and will do great in this situation.

In the final chapter, we will explore moments in your acting career that may be especially challenging for your self-confidence, and how to deal with such situations.

KEY POINTS

- "Imposter syndrome" is tied to feeling like a fraud and wondering when others will notice your inadequacy.

- You may experience imposter syndrome when your hard work finally pays off, such as when you get cast in a dream role.
- Alternatively, coming back to acting after a hiatus may also trigger this feeling.
- As your posture and what you say reflect your lack of self-confidence, your fears can turn into self-fulfilling prophecies.
- The inner critic often compounds the effects of imposter syndrome.
- Being aware of the tricks your mind can play on you, and having a range of targeted tools at your disposal, can help you overcome imposter syndrome.
- Talking to others about imposter syndrome can also lessen the strain and help you realize you are not alone.

CHAPTER 10

SELF-CONFIDENCE AND
THE ACTING LIFE

Becoming a self-confident actor does not happen overnight.

It is the result of a gradual process of learning how to nurture your self-confidence day by day, one small step at a time.

Some situations present especially good opportunities for working on your self-confidence.

In this final chapter, we will explore various challenging situations that you can use as an opportunity for growth.

The goal in exploring these situations is to start thinking how to apply the tools you have learned to nurture your self-confidence even when feeling under pressure.

SELF-CONFIDENCE BEFORE AUDITIONS

Before an audition is the most obvious time when you need an extra self-confidence boost.

You are pitted against many other hopefuls, some of them with more credits to their name, and your performance is evaluated by industry professionals.

As if this was not nerve-wracking enough, auditions are hard to come by, depending on where you live, especially in the early days of your acting career.

As a result, whenever a casting opportunity presents itself, the stakes are sky-high.

Because of all these factors, your natural playfulness as an actor, which leads to the best performances, can get stifled by this high-pressure atmosphere.

In addition, it is hard to give a memorable performance when you only have a few brief moments to show off your skills.

However, with the right mindset, it is possible to make the most of any audition, even in the most difficult circumstances.

Here are a few points that are worth remembering:

The casting team is on your side

Even though it may be hard to believe, the members of the casting team are rooting for you to be great.

If you are, and you are right for the part, that will make their job so much easier.

Keep this in mind as you go through the audition process: they want you to do well. All you have to do is show them who you are and why you are right for the part.

Take the long-term view

Don't treat this audition as a one-off, but as a way to build an ongoing working relationship with the people watching your performance.

The members of the casting team are in this industry for the long haul, and so are you.

Don't worry about getting this part. Focus on giving the best performance you can, regardless of the outcome.

Use your performance as an opportunity to provide the casting team with a taste of what you can offer as an actor.

Prioritize your self-confidence

Remember "mirror neurons:" the more confident you are, the more those watching you will have confidence in you.

Even if you are not right for this part, a confident performance makes you stand out in the minds of the casting team as a contender for future opportunities.

So make sure you give the most confident performance you can.

Remember that you are unique

Even though some of the other actors auditioning for this role may have a similar look, you are unique.

You bring your own set of qualities and life experiences to the table. There is nobody like you in the entire world.

Whether or not you are right for this part, focus on showing up just as you are, with your uniqueness on full display.

Do your best and forget the rest

Keep in mind what is in your control and outside your control.

You cannot control whether you are right for this part or who else is in the running.

However, you *can* control how well you prepare.

This includes arriving on time, learning your lines, as well as researching the director, the company, the location, and the specific project.

Being well prepared in all these different ways will provide a solid foundation for your self-confidence.

SELF-CONFIDENCE AND FIRST DAY INSECURITIES

You may think that if you get cast, all your self-confidence problems will be over.

However, when you turn up for the table read, first day rehearsals, or anything that qualifies as your first day on the job, new insecurities are likely to raise their head.

"New level, new devil," as the saying goes.

You may obsess over not being right for the job,

who would be better suited, and so on–classic symptoms of "imposter syndrome."

If you find yourself in this situation, remember that your fear of being found out is caused by your negativity bias; you are not a fraud.

Start noticing moments when your brain is distorting the way you see yourself and challenge any self-critical thoughts that arise.

In addition, make a list of all the reasons you deserve this opportunity.

Putting these reasons in writing is a powerful way to re-direct your attention to the arguments in your favor.

Remember the positivity ratio. For every self-critical thought, find four positive thoughts to counteract it.

Talk about your imposter syndrome with close friends or a therapist.

They will remind you of all the reasons you deserve the good things that are coming your way.

You are so close to having what you want. Accept that you are good enough and stop getting in your own way.

Come to your first day well-rested, prepared, having done your research, and learned your lines.

By taking all these steps, you are setting yourself up for success.

SELF-CONFIDENCE AFTER NOTES

Getting notes should not undermine your self-confidence, but this happens all too frequently.

One important reason is that when the director and other members of the production team watch your performance, their perceptions are influenced by the negativity bias.

As a result, they are likely to focus a disproportionate amount of their attention on all the aspects of your performance that are not working, while ignoring what you are doing well.

In addition, most notes are given in the run-up to opening night, when everyone is frazzled.

At such stressful times, every hint of criticism is likely to trigger your negativity bias more than usual, making you doubt yourself.

To protect your self-confidence, make a list of all the things you are doing well.

In writing this list, remember the positivity ratio.

Look for at least four things you did well for every piece of criticism you receive.

You could also ask your fellow actors what they enjoyed about your performance, and return the favor by giving them some positive feedback.

In addition, do not suffer in silence. Talk to your fellow actors about how the notes you received are making you feel about yourself.

They are probably struggling with their own self-doubts, and it makes sense to lean on each other for support. This will help you relieve stress and gain perspective.

Taking these steps will counteract the harmful effects that notes may have on your self-confidence.

Protecting your mental health will also allow you to take the criticism constructively, which will help you improve your performance.

SELF-CONFIDENCE AFTER PUBLIC CRITICISM

Public criticism could come from various sources, such as professional reviews of your work or social media postings from audience members.

Even if you decide not to read the reviews, it is hard to avoid seeing online comments that criticize your work.

In today's social media environment, everyone

is a critic, and for stage actors, every night is press night.

As there are so many ways in which criticism can come your way, you need strategies to protect your self-confidence.

The better prepared you are, the more you can take control of your mental health and prevent criticism from affecting your performance.

Of course, the easiest way to reassure yourself is to remind yourself that criticism is often just a matter of taste.

Not everyone will resonate with the show or your choices; that is to be expected.

If everyone enjoyed the same things, there would be no variety, and our world would be far less interesting.

It is also helpful to remind yourself, if you are hurting because of a particular piece of criticism, that the negativity bias amplifies your negative feelings.

We often only focus on the one negative aspect mentioned in a comment, even if that comment contains many pieces of praise.

Now that you are aware of the negativity bias, and that being an actor makes you turn this negativity bias towards yourself, you may find it easier to comfort yourself.

Over time, you will become more skilled at protecting your self-confidence when facing public criticism.

SELF-CONFIDENCE AFTER PUBLIC HUMILIATION

Perhaps you forgot your lines in the middle of a show, in a way that was obvious to every audience member.

Or maybe something deeply embarrassing about you went viral on social media—and now you have to perform in front of people who have probably seen it.

Whatever the source of your public humiliation, this experience is likely to feel isolating and can knock your self-confidence in a big way.

If you find yourself in this situation, it is worth realizing that most successful actors have faced some form of public humiliation over the course of their career.

You are not alone; it is simply your turn to face this ordeal.

Use every tool you have learned in this book,

and anything else that has worked for you in the past.

You will get through this; you just have to turn up, as well prepared as possible, and place your entire focus on your performance, instead of worrying about anything else.

Here is the good news: the first time you deal with this kind of situation will probably feel the worst.

After that, you won't fear it as much. You will know that you managed to get through it in the past.

It may be difficult to see this experience in a positive light when you are in the midst of it, but in the long run, this situation is an opportunity to overcome shame.

Use this opportunity well. You've got this.

SELF-CONFIDENCE WHEN DEALING WITH UNEMPLOYMENT

Periods of unemployment are a frequent occurrence in an actor's life.

You may go through times when you struggle to find acting work, and times when you may even struggle to find bill-paying work outside of acting.

Being unemployed as an actor is nothing to be ashamed of.

Although it is a challenging experience, it is also worth noting that unemployment is a rite of passage in the acting community.

Especially in the early days, unemployment is a badge of belonging.

As you are likely to find yourself in this situation many times over the course of your acting career, it is worth learning how to deal with unemployment in a healthy way.

The better you learn to deal with it, the better your mental health will be, which will improve your chances of finding acting work in the future.

Your brain chemistry when you are not working as an actor will be different from when you are performing.

Nothing can replace the adrenaline you get every time you perform on stage, nor the sense of pride when you receive the audience's applause.

If your most recent acting work was in film or TV, your brain probably misses the buzz of activity that comes with being on set.

However much you miss performing, it is worth keeping in mind that creativity is cyclical, and periods of unemployment are the low-activity part of that cycle.

This seemingly empty time is essential; see it for the opportunities it presents.

Do not spend this precious time worrying. Use it to recharge your energy.

Spend time with friends and find joy in every little gift that life offers: a rainbow, a ray of sunshine, a flower making its way through the cracks in the stony ground.

Here are a few things you can do to turn this period of inactivity as an actor into an opportunity for growth:

- Develop a sustainable self-care routine
- Read self-help books on relevant topics
- Put together your own acting projects
- Work on new skills to add to your acting CV
- Find bill-paying work that fits around your acting-related activities

CONCLUSION

Throughout this book, you have developed a complex understanding of your negativity bias, which is at the root of low self-confidence as an actor.

Although the negativity bias is excellent at keeping you safe from dangers within your environment, it can become a problem if you turn it against yourself.

Based on the positivity ratio, you pay four times more attention to self-critical than to positive thoughts you have about yourself.

As such, turning your negativity bias against yourself distorts your sense of self and damages your self-confidence.

Because of the many insecurities that come

with being an actor, you are at particular risk of turning your negativity bias against yourself, especially as you get better at your craft.

To improve your self-confidence as an actor, you need to get into the habit of using your brain as an ally instead of allowing it to become your enemy. This requires conscious effort.

Counteracting the effects of your negativity bias on your sense of self requires you to start thinking differently–this takes time and practice.

The more you practice, the better you will get at identifying negative self-talk and using the tools you have learned to counteract its effects.

You will also get better at calming your amygdala before you perform, to prevent nerves getting in the way.

By nurturing your self-confidence, you increase your chances of having a successful acting career and great mental health.

As you apply everything you have learned in this book to your acting career, you will also start using these insights and tools in other parts of your life.

These skills will not just improve your self-confidence as an actor–they will enhance your whole life.

You are unique, and so are your needs. The tools in this book are only a starting point for you to develop your own process.

Keep experimenting and tailor the tools to your specific requirements.

Finally, please consider passing on this knowledge to any actor friends who may be struggling with their self-confidence.

They will benefit and be happier for it, and you will become a beacon of strength and empowerment in their lives.

I wish you all the best with your acting career.

———

I would like to ask you for a small favor.

Reviews are the best way to spread the word about this book. If you have found this book helpful, it would mean a lot to me if you could leave a review.

Even if you write only a sentence or two, it will help. Thank you!

GET A FREE BOOK

If you want to improve your chances of success as an actor, psychology can help.

Psychology Tools for Actors teaches you ten simple yet powerful psychology tools to take your acting career to the next level.

Download for free when you sign up for the *Psychology for Actors* newsletter at:

www.psychologyforactors.com/newsletter

ABOUT THE AUTHOR

Alexa Ispas holds a PhD in psychology from the University of Edinburgh.

The books in her *Psychology for Actors Series* provide actors with proven psychology techniques to thrive and build a successful career.

If you'd like to stay in touch with Alexa, and learn more psychological tools that are directly relevant to actors, please sign up for the *Psychology for Actors* newsletter. You will receive a short free book when you sign up.

You can sign up for the newsletter and receive your free book at:

www.psychologyforactors.com/newsletter

Memorization for Actors

Self-Confidence for Actors

Resilience for Actors

Motivation for Actors

Excellence for Actors

Success for Actors

For more information, please visit:

www.psychologyforactors.com

Made in the USA
Las Vegas, NV
23 December 2024

15241998R00069